READ BETWEEN THE LINES

Volume 2

A collection by

Rhoda Chaalan

Please do not do anything for me,
you plan to use against me in the
future. Please do not do something
for me to get recognition. Please do
not do anything for me to make me
feel like I owe you. Please do not do
anything for me if your intention is to
want to own me. Please do not help
me, to say my personal success is
because of you.

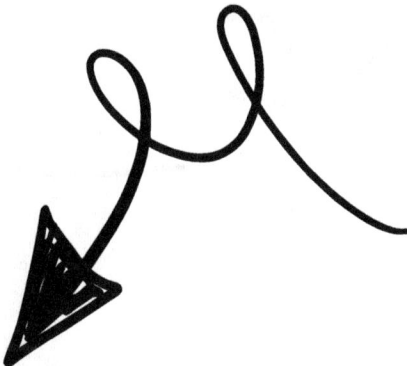

I am a high achiever and over-analyser. I am great under pressure and I procrastinate. I know I am capable and quite insecure. I am so driven and fear embarrassment. I am social and I love being alone. I am all of these things and more.

Careful of the wording used in describing yourself, for the universe will hear you. If you are drained, you will feel it. If you say you are anxious, you will become it. Take control of your mind, and past habits. Change your way of thinking. Trick your mind, and watch what the body will do. You are in charge of how you will feel today.

I know that you are lying, and the

words coming out of your mouth

are not helping. I'll let you think

that I believe you, In fact, I'll even

apologize. But slowly I am

handing you the rope, try not to

hang yourself.

I digest my emotional wounds

and release my expectations.

I want to be repaired.

I reflect on what happened,

I am angry.

But I know I will emerge

stronger,

I will be more alive, more

empowered than

I ever was before.

My comfort zone will allow my

personality, to change around

different people.

I have yet to give all of myself to one

person.

How poignant that would be.

*The time has come
to venture
forward, Do not
let fear turn your
eyes back.
You left all that
behind for a reason.*

I have to take a journey

back in time. Into the

past I go. I need to lose

my mind, in order to find

my soul.

When I am in conversation with my
friend about my past, I realise how naive
I am. I didn't realise this until I spoke
the words out loud about how ill-treated
I was. Listening to myself speak, made it
all sink in.

When the abuser plays victim. You have a vengeful abuser who will not only hurt you physically but emotionally and mentally. This person is most dangerous and will not stop, he will play weak when needed; he will try to rob your justice.

They take advantage of the fact, that you have a family bond. They use the words loving and respectful, to manipulate and hurt you, because they know you. For you will find it awfully hard, to remove yourself because you are family, because for you, family is a strong word. But this negative energy you need to escape, they will drain you of your happiness. Constantly creating drama, at your expense. You need to take close evaluation, life will be better, by letting go of these poisonous family members. Cutting ties and walking away forever, your health, happiness and peace of mind must come first.

Try not to interrupt when people tell you what they are going through. Let them speak, listen to them. Don't rush to compare your experience to theirs. Even if they are similar, don't offer unsolicited advice. Practise to listen and understand, and not to respond. Sometimes they just want to be heard. All they want to do is vent.

There will be people who will give you flowers, and there will be people who will give you love. Let love be the seed that allows the flower to bloom.

Tell me the truth about you.

Don't hide your past pains,

even if it embarrasses you.

Let me learn from your mistakes.

Your confidence in speaking up inspires me.

You speak honestly of

how you feel and how you got up,

you show me that growth is possible,

even when the going gets tough.

Have I not told you how sorry I am? That I let you down? I let fear take control of you, and didn't show you hope. I let you think that this was how life will always be. I'm sorry that you were too busy giving love to others, and it was draining you. You gave away your time and energy, and helped so many people. I'm sorry they never appreciated you. I'm sorry I wasn't there, when you cried yourself to sleep. I'm sorry I didn't give you strength to get up and leave. I'm sorry I made you think that you were alone. I'm sorry that I made you feel you should worry, about what others would think of you. I'm sorry that you felt you had a reputation to uphold. I'm sorry that in all you did, it was to help others.

I'm sorry I played with your self-esteem and made you feel less. I'm sorry that I betrayed you and left you in a mess. I'm sorry I didn't push you harder, I'm sorry I didn't kill the fear. I'm sorry that you didn't get to be what you wanted to be. I'm sorry I didn't love you when you needed me most. I'm sorry I isolated you; I wish I could turn back time. I'm sorry that I let you down. I'm sorry I didn't let you live a moment of peace, when your body and soul were mine.

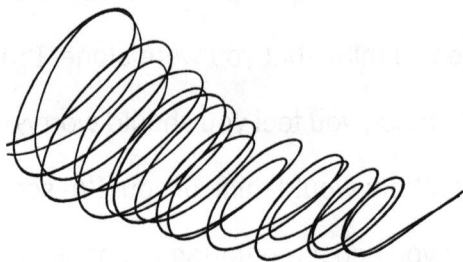

Why is it a stranger gives me more

support, than those who are close

to me? Why is it that those who

were once close cannot

comprehend my success?

They are used to seeing me being broken,

and somehow This made them feel better.

I don't understand how they wouldn't be

my biggest support knowing what I went

through and how I got here.

A comfort for those who were once close

was knowing you were broken, alone and

hurt. The minute that changed, the jealousy

took hold, like a snake: to know a broken

person can heal and be strong, causes many

people feel little and no longer belong.

I could go around and buy things I never had.

Instead, I will teach people things I was

never taught. A neglected childhood, teaches

you to love unconditionally, protect more,

love more. It also allows you to appreciate

what knowledge can show you, what time

can give you. The desire for material

possession is just a want, the true definition

of living is appreciating what you have.

Understanding the needs from the want and

always giving back.

When things in life get tough, people in life
tend to run. The strongest of relationships
walk hand in hand through a battlefield,
unarmed. Let love be your armour and
faith be your sword. Don't give up because
it is easier to leave, instead try to stay and
make it work. Do not let pride be the
burden, that leaves you alone wounded.
Battle the war together, you have more of
a chance winning it together than alone.

In all you do, don't lose who you are. If you

feel the need to speak up, speak up! If you

feel the need to make a change, make

change happen! If you feel the need that

something needs to be done, do it!

Lead by example.

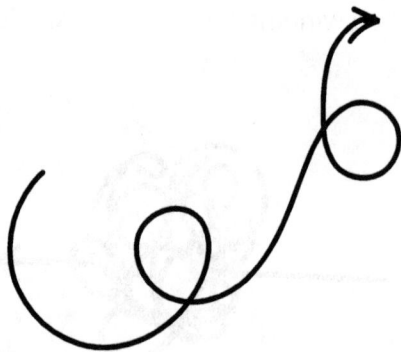

You cannot save me.
I am not ready to be rescued.
When the time comes,
I will let you know.
Until then,
stay close to me.
Keep reminding me that I matter.

It's funny
how culturally we demean divorce,
as if I would settle for any man.
They think I should be grateful,
that a man would even look my way,
being what they think is broken,
and my offspring, they see as baggage.
Let me tell you my opinion,
I throw this cultural belief away.
I am more valuable than when I was a virgin,
I have children who are a gift.
I refuse to settle,
I will only take the best.
If you can't be a man,
who is a good role model, mentor,
and an example to my kids,
don't bother even trying.
Because as much as it is about me,
the way you treat me,
the way you care,
my boys will mimic you as they grow.

So, I will be certain,

that I will not settle.

I will not accept a man who is still broken,

Heal yourself.

Love yourself.

And until then,

stay away from single mothers.

We are ok with being on our own!

Don't tell me the truth of my past,
for I built a great illusion
and told people an exceptional story.
The truth will destroy my illusion.

Please do not assume my mind is dirty.

Clearly,

you mean I have a

very sexy imagination.

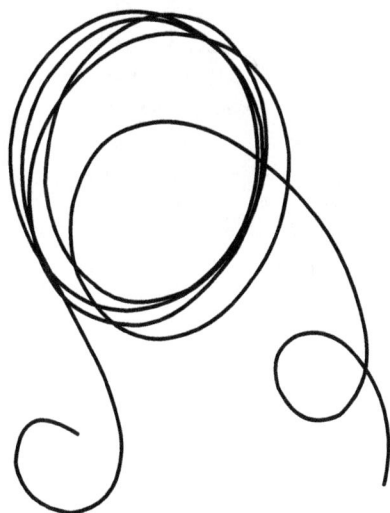

Your money does not impress me.

Your job status means nothing to

me. Show me human kindness,

that will amaze me.

With every past pain and every heartache. With every life experience, it's all wisdom I gain.

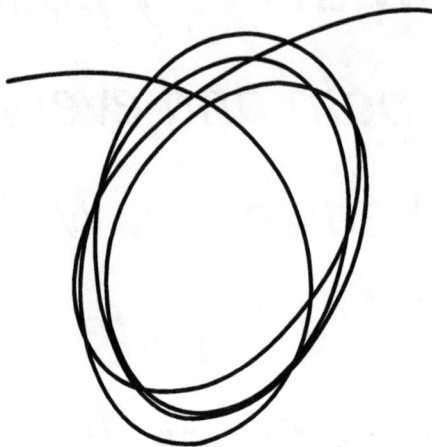

Do not desire the fancy and expensive.

Look at the product and make your

decision. The price tag doesn't mean

prestige, It's how you hold yourself in

what you wear that speaks.

When she spoke,
she silenced my anger.
She made all the hate go away,
the anxiety disappeared.

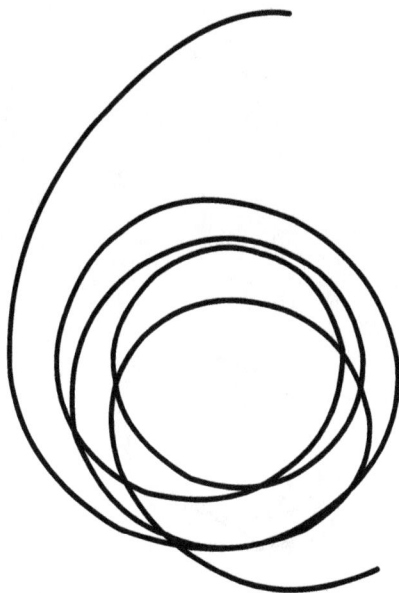

To be absorbed by pain, is to distract yourself, as though the pain is non-existent. Both will leave the heart wounded. Pain is persistent if not properly dealt with.

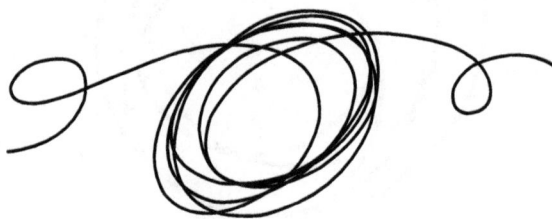

I need to find a solution to it all. The solution

needs to be now.

I need all the answers and to find a way. This is

my anxiety, of trying to solve everything every

single day.

When I stop to breathe and write down what I

need to do, I realise that it was my mind

playing a trick or two.

I smile quietly and take another breath in.

I've got this. It's easy.

I just need to take it day by day.

Remember: you can't take back words that

have escaped your mouth, But also remember

that sometimes,

they needed to be said.

I have wanted to run away, To get up
and leave. Escape. The dream of
wanting to start all over, a fresh,
wonderful start. New beginning. It's ok
to feel like this. It only means that you
have been selfless for too long and it's
ok to start to be a little selfish.

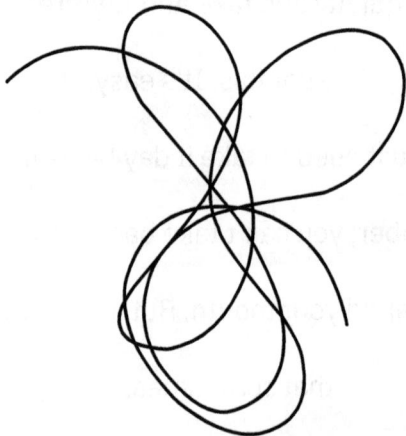

My perspective,
my actions,
and my values,
are my biggest
challenges.

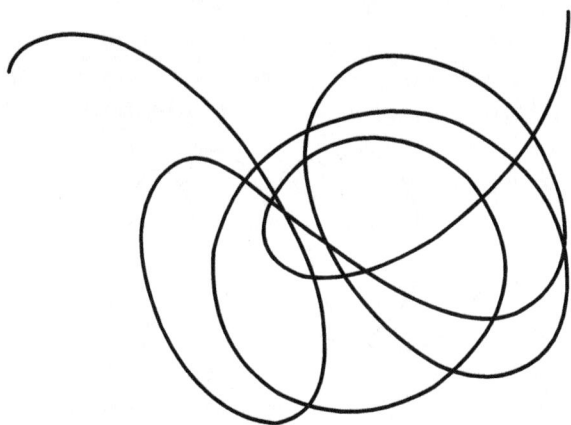

By pleasing people,
you could lose yourself and who you really are.
It's okay to lose people,
they can be replaced.
But losing yourself
does more damage than good.

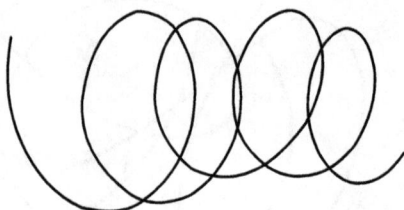

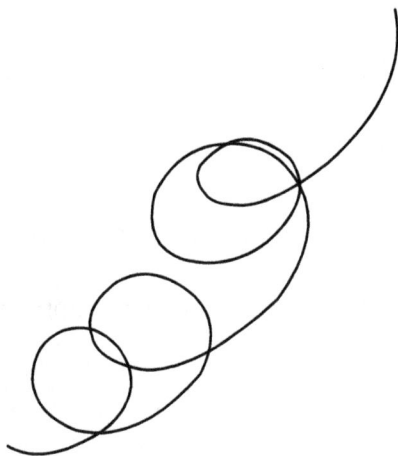

If I speak of my loved ones, in a moment of

anger, do not interfere. Do not agree or make

a comment, for in seconds, it will turn on you,

for the anger between one's own blood does

not last. But the anger between that of me

and a stranger, can go on forever.

One perspective, two perspectives, three perspectives, four. The additional perspectives you receive, gives value to your realization so much more.

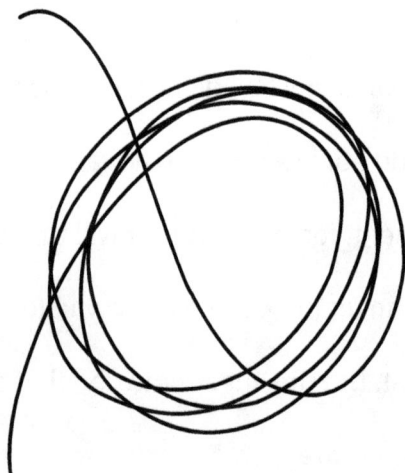

The shoemaker
works so hard,
that his children stay barefoot.
The chef cooks up a feast,
while his children are hungry.
An author writes her books,
while her children never read.

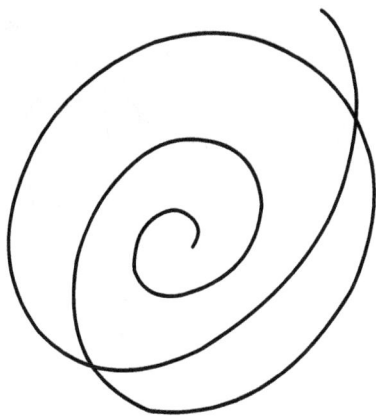

I bite my tongue,
hold back my opinion.
I take a deep breath in,
that one moment of patience,
that moment of anger,
I saved myself moments of regret.
You go to the circus
to watch the clown,
so, don't blame the clown
for playing his role.
If you don't like it,
stop going to the circus.

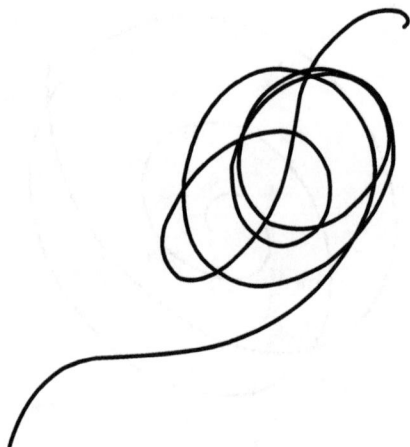

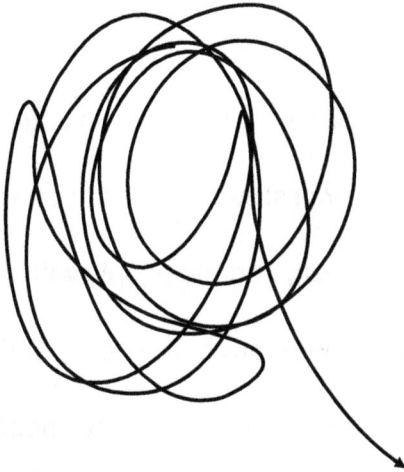

I needed a hero.

A real person on demand,

I needed some guidance.

Someone who would stay with me to

the end,

I needed a hero.

So, I became one,

I'm my own best friend.

Weak people will play victim, strong people will strive. Intelligent people will succeed, humble people will never forget where they came from. Work in silence and let your achievements speak volumes.

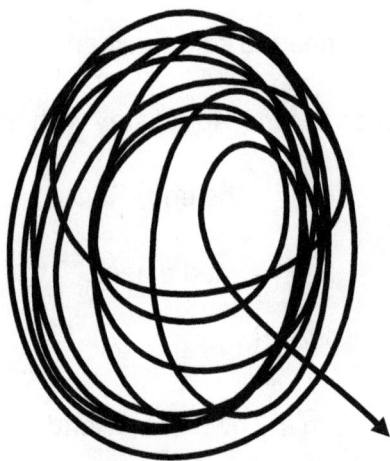

Make the change in the way you see things,and watch how you see things that you used to look at change.

Let building a wonderful reputation come naturally, keep your name clean, don't make compromises. Don't think about material stuff or being successful, focus on what changes you can make, to make the world better. This is the ultimate legacy you can leave behind.

They sat and ate at the family table together. They held each other a little tighter, prayed a little more. They sat with their thoughts, which in real time they could never do. They let music heal the pain. They showed their young ones strength. The realisation of what really matters took place. The grey cloud stayed a while, but with it came lessons. They never saw things the same. Being content was no longer about money, prestige, or fame. For they knew each person who had lost a loved one, would do anything for that time back again.

Sometimes the smallest step in the right direction, ends up being the biggest step of your life. Tiptoe if you must, but take that step regardless.

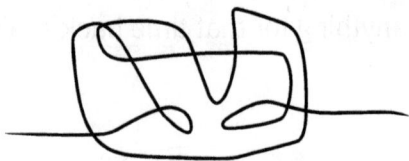

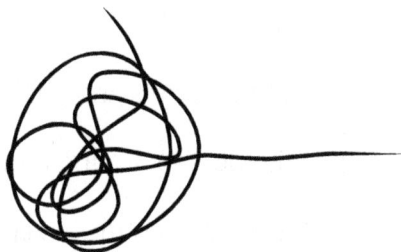

Strength is in not giving up,

it's achieving your goals,

and, above all,

walking continuously with God.

With strength comes the power of

accomplishments,

With faith, your perceptions change.

with God by your side,

you are always winning.

My past is just that. Money is
something that comes and goes, and
I choose the people around me. But
none of those have control over me.

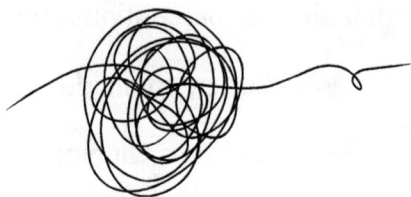

Money is less important than people. If it became more important, then people would be worthless.

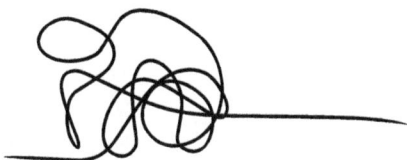

A man sat wondering, who it is that he

loves. Seeing two women was hard

enough. One that he constantly lied to, and

the other he was completely honest with.

One that lived out his desires, The other,

the mother of his children he required.

Which woman is it that this man loves?

You are of great importance. Your

internal organs are the same as the

person next to you.

If you are lost, you will find your way.

If you feel down, you will rise again.

If you are hurting, you will find hope.

If you are sad,

you will find happiness again.

These are just passing phases,

like the moon.

You are of great importance.

Do not doubt this to be true.

I fear the unknown,
embrace me.
I fear the dark,
hold me.
I fear the unknown,
guide me.
I fear falling in love,
catch me.

I can easily unfriend you.

Uncousin you.

Unco-worker you. Unfollow you. Even un-

family you. Don't drain my soul, I don't need

your toxic traits. I'll take control. I don't

have time to debate.

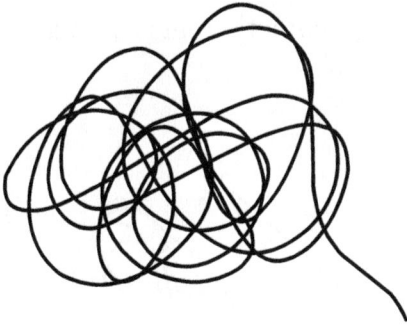

Nothing is wrong with a little banter, a little

flirting. A little laugh here and there, we are

both well aware it will go nowhere.

As long as it's innocent,

I'm happy to play along.

After all, I miss the verbal comebacks of a

character that is strong.

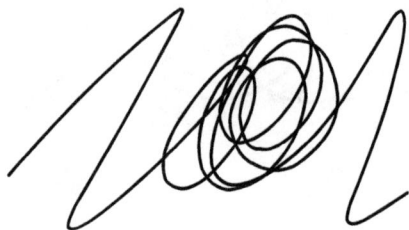

Single parents don't have an outlet.
A partner to go to, to tell of things their kids
have done during the day.
Things that have made them proud, things that
have made them laugh, things that have made
them cry.
So, when a single mum opens up about her
kids, don't automatically change into
competitive mode.
Which in a way, is kind of a compliment to the
single mum.
But unfortunately for you, that is not where her
head is at.
For her to open up and say something about her
kids is hard enough, because she doesn't want
to boast or be judged.
She truly just wanted to share and be heard.

Be a friend that finds pride in other peoples' joy, not the stealer of their thunder. That is all.

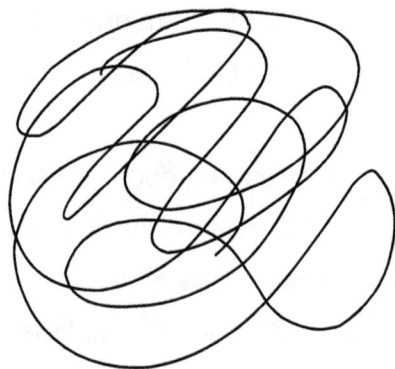

You belong. You don't have to do it
all now. Pace yourself. What you're
creating is of great meaning, not
everyone has to understand or
appreciate it. You can choose to
make today a great one, you are
loved.

I am greatness

All of my past has contributed to the person I

am today.

I am in control of what I need and what I want.

I am in control of getting to where I want to go.

My empire is within.

My personal worth is humbleness.

I am a source of energy that not only does my

best but drives others to do so too.

I am me.

I am accepting of myself and loving myself.

I am greatness.

"I'm afraid," her hands slightly shaking. She
had no idea what she was feeling, she
couldn't move, the fear of the past
suffocating her.

He knew at that moment; she was the one.

Life experience had shown him this. With
both hands, he forced her up against the
wall, his eyes fiercely looking into hers, heart
racing

"You don't think I'm not afraid?" he responded.

Both were vulnerable.

Both deeply hoping they will not be
hurt again.

A lie may have

expired early, but

the scars will last a

long time.

The problem of a lie
is time.
Every lie has an expiry date.

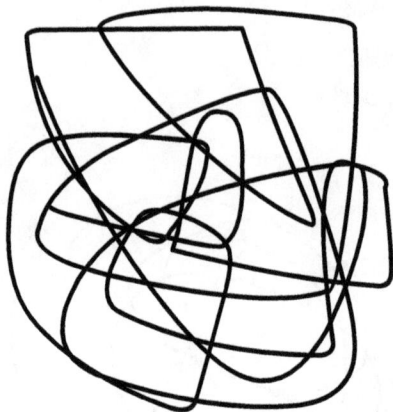

When they scream,
talk to them.
When they yell, calm them down.
Be better than them.
Do not feed them what they feed you.
Don't give them the satisfaction.

Whether confident in myself or not,

I'll let you know when you look good.

When you smell good, when you have

made a change, I will let you know.

Insecure jealous people will never

compliment you, they feel it will give

you power.

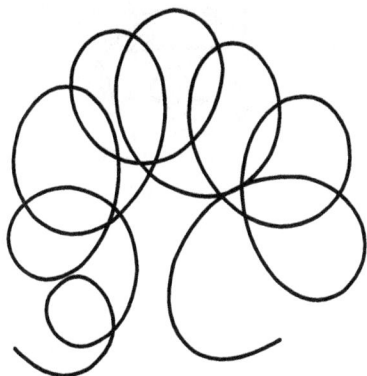

They say fake it
until you make it.
I say if you dreamed it,
planned it,
worked for it,
and never given up on it,
you've already made it.
Making it is not about richness.
It's about personal fulfillment.

Do not push back the
fears of the mind.
Dreams of the heart
wish to take the lead
and that's how you
grow.

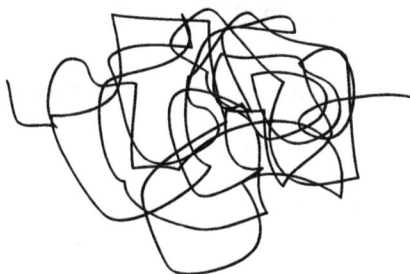

None of us are born with readymade

instructions, for the use of the brain.

Despite all of this, we have effective

ways to achieve what we want, both in

work and personal life, using intellectual

resources.

One can follow their dreams and

conquer hardship, and use the

maximum potential of their personality.

I allowed you to think I was failing

when I was climbing the ladder of

success.

You preferred a victim, but that I

could not be.

I revealed my true self when the

time was right, Now, your

conscience will be speaking as you

lay your head, alone at night.

In school, you trust in the teacher. At home, you feel the protection of your parents.

On the plane, you know the pilot will be a person of conviction. On a ship, you have faith in the captain.

On a train, you have confidence in the driver.

So, in life imagine you had the same trust, protection, confidence, faith, and conviction in God How calmer life would be?

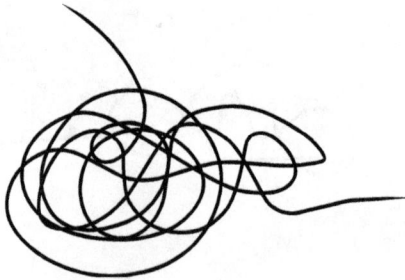

Be firm,
but not rude.
Be humble, but not timid.
Be proud, but not vain.
Be kind, but not weak.
Be wise, but not foolish.
Be loving,
but don't be taken advantage of.

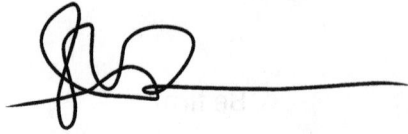

Many will not be able to comprehend

my past.

Many would not last a day in my shoes.

Many are left confused about the

weight I carry.

But many will give their unneeded

opinion.

A person who has not experienced

hardship, can only sit back and listen.

For their opinion holds no strength.

In my journey, I look out for those who are: happy for my happiness, sad for my sadness, the person who cheers me on in my absence.

When you wish to talk badly of

someone,

let them be there to defend

themselves.

Doing so in their absence, says more

about you,

than the person you are talking

about.

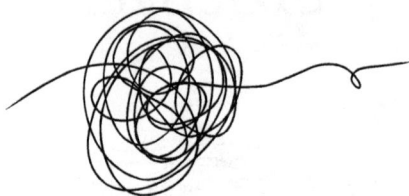

As I sit and tell you a story,
be prepared that this is not the only story
you will hear,
you will get mini conversations, other stories
and a joke,
that makes me laugh,
all added into one.

People will love the idea of you. They will love the benefits of knowing you but they will lack the maturity to handle the reality of you. As you grow, they will shrivel.

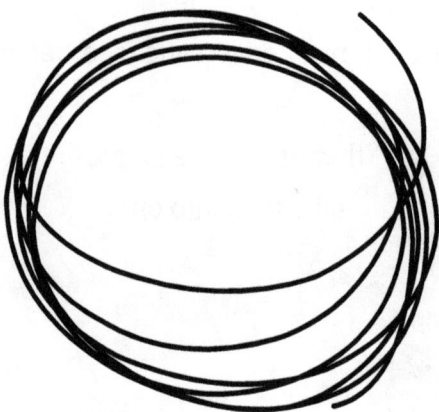

The fairy tale of fitting into the glass slipper, has made our girls feel that a prince is what makes them happy. But the happiness lies on the shattered glass ceiling, where this girl can eventually have her own way. Her own happy ending.

I crave you

in the most innocent form.

I crave my head laying on your chest,

as the beat of your heart

synchronises with mine.

I crave our arm around me,

where I feel an armour of protection.

I crave you gently stroking my hair,

snuggling closer

and closer as my fears begin to vanish.

I crave being vulnerable,

and letting you see the real me.

I crave being your one and only.

I crave my perplexed heart letting someone

hold me.

No visible symptoms, just a head full of darkness. No fracture, sprains, or broken bones, just voices speaking as if he were a clone. A smile still embedded in a society, where men are wrongly taught to mask their emotions. He wants to get better, and makes it his devotion. The family is in agony, as he no longer answers his phone. Before you know it, the family is picking out a gravestone.

An ounce of blood is worth more than
a pound of friendship.
A pound of friendship that becomes
family, is worth more than a ton of
companions.

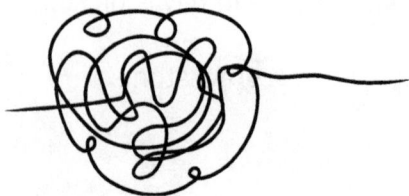

Imagine being strong enough
not to have to tell your side of the story,
having nothing to prove to anyone,
and having full support in the process.

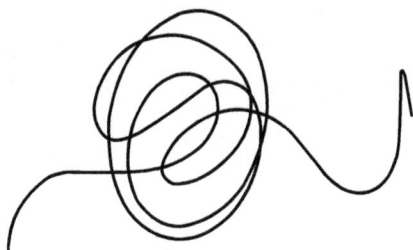

You must not listen
to naysayers.
No one can tell you what you can,
or can't do,
or what is possible.

Don't do what you don't like, live
your life doing what you love. Be the
catalyst that helps others connect,

with the infinite side of their nature.

Help create extraordinary results in all
areas of their lives. Be the catalyst that
walks the talk,

and is devoted to making a difference.

When you try and
please everybody,
the first person you
let down is
yourself.

www.ingramcontent.com/pod-product-compliance
Lightning Source LLC
Chambersburg PA
CBHW071851090426
42811CB00004B/570